Disclaimer

No part of this work may be reproduced or transmitted in any form or by any means, electronic or mechanical, including photocopying, recording or by any information storage or retrieval system, without the written permission of the copyright owner.

Every precaution has been taken to ensure that the information presented here is accurate.

However, neither the authors shall have any liability nor any person or entity concerning any loss or damage caused or alleged to be caused directly or indirectly by the information contained within this book. The information is presented as on as-is-basis. There are no guarantees. This is an information product. Everyone is different- we all have different approaches, background, discipline, and lifestyle, so we cannot guarantee any form of income with this met

hod due to this. The amount of profits made depends solely on the individual. You agree that we are not responsible for your failure or success. You may not reprint or resell this material

Introduction

This book is going to be a quick read as we want you to take actionable steps after reading this book. You do not have to wait for eternity to find out the ways to increase profits in your business.

You can find profits in any part of your business like in Sales, Purchases, Admin Expenses, and Taxes. We have organized information by such topics. Again, the information has been divided into fast impact areas and strategy.

So you can take away the action points from fast impact areas, and you can see results in your business in 24 to 48 hours, and when it comes to strategy, results will take a longer time to show up.

Hope you enjoy the book.

Turnaround Business in 24 Hours- Is It Possible?

Whatever might be the reason for you to pick this book, one thing is for sure that you want to increase the profits of your business. You must be asking yourself that is it possible to turnaround the company so quickly? Some of the techniques discussed in this book will give an immediate boost to your business, and some will take time. Also if you own a large business, the percentage of the increase in profit will not be so high, but the impact will be huge. On the other hand in a small business, you can see the substantial increase in profits immediately.

Also, some of the strategies/techniques might apply to big businesses, and some might apply to small business.

Table of Contents

Chapter 1 1

Sale Transactions-The Key to Kingdom of Heaven and Avalanche of Profits 1

Identify Revenue Leakages and Taking Corrective Action 2

Online Revenue Leakages 7

Point of Sale (Up-Selling and Cross-Selling) 10

Increase in Prices 10

Clearing Old Inventories 11

Offering Low-end Products or Services to Old Leads 11

Cash discount 12

Case Study 1.1 12

Strategy – 14

Expanding Distribution Platforms and Making Use of References 14

Chapter 2 15

Purchase Transactions-When You Spend Carefully, You Save and Increase Profits 15

Terms agreed with the Suppliers 16

Case Study 2.1 17

Case Study 2.2 18

Discount Policy 19

Annual Discount or Incentives 19

Strategy – 20

Consolidation of Purchase 20

Case Study 2.3 21

Chapter 3 22

Working Capital Management 22

Case Study 3.1 ……………………………...26

Chapter 4 27

Spend Wisely on Sales and Marketing Activities and See How Your Business Grows 27

Change The Bidding Method 28

Focus on Local Marketing not Generic SEO 28

Measure the Sales and Marketing Effort 29

Chapter 5 31

Why You Should Not See Taxman As Your Enemy- He Can Also Make You Rich 31

Slash Corporate Income Tax by Almost 30% When You Hire an Employee 32

Bills You Pay Add Money to Bank Account 34

Case Study 5.1 ……………………………….35

When You Train Your Employees-You Save Tax Upto 50% 36

When You Export-You Get Additional Benefit Up To 5% 37

Case Study 5.2 38

Starting a New Business Can Save a Ton of Tax . 39

- Chapter 6 40
- Other Areas of Savings 40
- When You Barter You Profit 40
- Telephone/Lease Line Bills-How to Identify Overbilling and Save Costs 42
- Travel Expense-Things to Do to Save Cost 43
- Bonus Chapter 45
- What You Can Learn From Competitors 45
- Expenses Add Profits to Your Bank Account 46
- Is Your Business Suffering From Feast or Famine Cycle? 48
- About the Authors 52
- Compendium of Case Studies 54

Chapter 1

Sale Transactions-The Key to Kingdom of Heaven and Avalanche of Profits

A sale is the life-line of any business. You ask any business owner they will agree with it. Without it, no business can survive.

To increase profits, we have divided into two areas

<u>Fast Impact Areas</u>

- Identify Revenue Leakages and corrective action to be taken
- Online revenue leakage and corrective action to be taken
- Point of Sale (Up Selling & Cross Selling)
- Increase in Price
- Clearing Old Inventories
- Selling low-end products or services to old leads
- Cash Discount

Strategy

- Growth in Volume of Sales through Expanding Distributorship/Channels

Let's look at them in detail

Identify Revenue Leakages and Taking Corrective Action

Do you know a company loses up to 7% of its revenue on account of revenue leakage and fraud in the revenue process? If you can find these leakages to that extent, you increase the profits.

Some of the reasons are below:

No Billing/Less Billing for the Job Done: Most of the time any additional work performed post the issuance of a purchase order from the customer will be either missed or is billed short. This happens because there is no proper communication between the delivery team with billing team. It is recommended to have a system which documents such additional request from the customer.

Client Reimbursements: Most of the time, expenses are incurred on behalf of the client with a promise to be reimbursed for the same. Unfortunately, due to process errors either the reimbursement is not claimed in time or completely missed. It is recommended to have proper tracking of such expenses.

Outside Warranty Job Not Billed: In our experience, we have seen many times bill not raised for the extra work done outside of the warranty. It happens because lack of shared database which is accessible to both billing as well as operations team.

Price Revision Effect: There are situations, where management decides to revise the price of its products or services, which sales department may not fully aware of immediately.

This situation can be lead to tremendous loss of revenue.

For example, management decides to change the price of products effective midnight on account of changes in VAT rates. However, the sales team continues to bill at old rates as the price master data is not updated.

Contracts Not Renewed in Time: Large enterprises generally do not renew contracts in time. It can severally impact the working capital cycle. Just imagine you have supplied material in the hope that contract will renew on its own, and then your customer raises its eyebrow and says "We will only make the payment only when

Contract is renewed" leading to delays in payment by 60 to 90 days. It is recommended starting initiating the renewal process a month in advance.

Lack of Customer Feedback System: Today most of the contracts have a milestone payment terms. Customers make payment only after the work is approved.

However, to the contrary, vendor raises the bill on client assuming that he has performed the work properly and expects the client to pay the same on time. However, the client comes back and says "This was not done, and That was not done". In the whole process, the extra cost is incurred on account of delayed payments.

Invoices Not Raised on Time: This affects the entire working capital cycle which results in interest cost when funds have to be borrowed to meet the shortfall.

It is recommended to maintain a tracker, where all the open projects are listed, and invoices against those orders are mapped. Mapping is possible in an excel sheet or accounting software.

Corrective Actions:

List all the Sales orders which are yet to be fulfilled: List down all the sales orders which are open, and pending for completion. Find out the average days to complete the order. If the order is pending for a long time, then it is a sign that something is wrong. The following could have happened.

- Sales Invoice has not been raised despite completion of the work
- Customer has cancelled the order, but the company has failed to take note of it. All the expenses related to that order should be put to stop and expenses incurred till date on that order should be recovered from the customer.

Order to Cash: It is highly recommended to calculate the number of days taken to convert a sales order to invoice to cash. On the calculation, if you find that number is abnormally high, then you should dig deep to find out the real reason. Most of the times, sales are recorded to boost the sales incentives and rewards. This calculation will bring to light any discrepancies when compared to quarter to quarter or month to month.

Customer Wise Data: If in a business, where a customer buys frequently, then this data can bring to light if there are any missing invoices. All you have to do is to plot the sales number on a month to month basis by the customer. If you see the numbers are not consistent, you need to find out the reason.

In our experience, where the volume of sales transactions is high and the process is not completely automated, chances of the invoice not being raised are quite high.

This data will also reveal whether invoice to customers are at the right price or not. All you have to do is to divide the total sales value by the number of invoices raised in a given period.

Discount Master Data: With so much of competition, it is common for the companies to offer a discount on products. However having said this, a lot of times discount is given arbitrarily or at the discretion of the staff in the company. This practice can lead to many losses as it hits bottom-line directly.

Billing software should have the discount master-data, and the billing executive should not be able to edit it. Monthly review of the discount given to customers will bring out the discrepancies.

Online Revenue Leakages

Now, most of the businesses including service businesses accept payment online. With the ease of doing transactions, there are challenges which can eat away profits very quickly.

Some of the things that can be done to mitigate this risk are:

Refund Policy: Most of the online businesses, report refund rate between 15-25%. Therefore, it is imperative to have a refund policy to avoid fraudulent refund request. People buying a product or availing a service, and then asking for the refund is quite common. In such cases, refund policy can come to rescue, and save tons of money and heartburn.

Chargebacks: Sometimes, customers will dispute the credit or debit card transaction. In most of the countries, a customer can dispute transaction within 180 days from the date of the transaction. Therefore, there is a high probability that credit card companies can hold funds till such chargebacks are resolved.

This can put a lot of stress on working capital, and in the worst case, if you lose the dispute, the entire sale value becomes a loss. One of our clients lost 5% of revenue only on account of chargebacks. To avoid the chargebacks, ensure that there is proof of delivery of product or service. It could be a copy of invoice, receipt copy signed by the customer, and other relevant documents. Try to take written confirmation or an email that shows product or service has been delivered.

Misuse of Coupons: To attract customers, companies time to time issue discount coupons which have a validity period. Normally such coupons are valid for a day or maximum a week. Companies have their back-end system or use third party platforms to manage coupons and its validity.

So there is a high risk that if such coupons are not managed well, the company can run into huge losses. Mind you such coupons give the discount of anywhere from 5% to 75%, therefore, having strong controls regarding the coupon management process is a must. Some of the things you can do in this regard are

- Create discount coupon codes that expire quickly.
- Create discount coupon codes that are limited by number.

- Review the coupon redemption on a daily basis.
- Review the channels to distribute coupon codes, whether it is on the own website or aggregators or affiliates.
- Create discount codes by city and state. This way you can find out the sales where coupons have been misused.

Make the Registration Process a Robust One: Most of the users try different email ids to redeem the coupon multiple times. In such a scenario, it makes sense to have a unique mobile number as a condition to get registered. Another way to track this is looking for IP addresses. Most of the back-end systems support this. If somebody is trying to register multiple times from same IP address, then the registration should be blocked. You might annoy few customers, but in the long run, you will avoid losses.

Place a Limit on the Referral Code: Companies encourage their customers to refer their friends to them by offering them an incentive in the form of a coupon. In this process, they fail to limit the number of people who can be referred. For instance, this code could be shared on Facebook,

LinkedIn or other social media and can be used by the many people.

Point of Sale (Up-Selling and Cross-Selling)

Point of sale is a very old concept in any sales transaction, but actually, it is much underutilized in most of the businesses.

Most of the businesses do not use point of sale or upsell.

Let's say you are in the business of carpet cleaning or providing pest control services

After the delivery of service, you can go to the client and tell him that he might require services again in the future, so why not sign a maintenance contract, whereby every three months pest control is done, and you give 10% discount upfront.

Increase in Prices

This one is quite evident, but actually, it is quite laughable that most of the businesses are reluctant to raise the price of the product or services, and fearing that their customers will move away to the competitors.

Then we ask them, are your customers thrilled with your product or service?

Most of them answered yes, and increased their prices. For example, increase in price by 10% will increase profits substantially.

Clearing Old Inventories
This again is a time and tested method, but again underutilized

There are many businesses where the inventory has no real value. In that scenario, you can have a fire sale where you offer items at a huge discount. A lot of big brands do fire sale at festive times.

Offering Low-end Products or Services to Old Leads
All the businesses can apply this concept.

Take our business, for instance; we are in the business of Consulting, Outsourcing, Compliance, and Registration. As we provide a variety of services, we get many leads. There are some who are ready to avail services straight away and some who do not.

We go back to leads that have not availed our services, and offer them something at the lower spectrum of our services which is still very helpful to them. This way client experiences our services and then signs up for the premium services in future.

Cash discount

As you are aware cash discount is offered when the customer pays in advance within stipulated days. Discount is calculated by the billing software or manually.

Sometimes calculations can go wrong when there are so many transactions on a day to day basis. One of our clients paid 0.21 million extra in cash discount. Below is the case study

---

Case Study 1.1

Error in Cash Discount-Company had to Pay 0.21 Million

Background: Client was in the business of selling and buying garments. We were engaged to look at the existing process on discounting and billing and internal controls for financial transactions.

What We Did: We took the sales register for one year. Against the sales, we plotted the received amount. We then calculated number of days to receive the payment invoice wise. We also added a column, where cash discount was given. Then we looked at the report for the correctness of Cash discount.

Cont ...

> **Results:** Finally, it was concluded that the company paid close to excess of INR 0.21 Million. When we reported this to the client, then client agreed to it saying it was attributable to manual systems and lack of proper control. Basically, the system of giving cash discount was not formalized. Post this; we set up a discount master data in the accounting software at the customer level. So the moment there was an error in cash discount, the software sent out the alerts to responsible parties in the company. Since this company had a large volume of sales on daily basis, a review mechanism to review the cash discount on weekly basis was setup.
>
> Also for excess cash discount of INR 0.21 Million was subsequently recovered from the customers via debit note. With this information in hand, we also looked at cash flow statement of the client on month to month basis. Cash discount was given to plug the gap between the receivables and payables, and at times it was not necessary to really give a Cash discount. Mind you our client was giving on an average of 2% Cash Discount. We estimated that if the client had managed Cash Flow well, it could have avoided 0.202 Million of Cash Discount.
>
> **What We Can Learn from this:** It's a good idea to review the cash discount calculations on a monthly basis

If you can implement some of the methods discussed above in your business, you can see increase in your profits in as little as 24 hours to 48 hours.

Strategy – Expanding Distribution Platforms and Making Use of References

Expanding Distribution Platforms: Let's say right now you are selling your products on Amazon. Find other platforms like Amazon, an example of this could be Snapdeal or Flipkart. So basically, you are reaching to a broader audience, and there is an enormous potential for you to increase your sales. When you increase your sales, you tend to increase your profits.

References: They are the time-tested method of increasing the sales and profits.

So let's say you are selling clothes. The moment your customer buys the Merchandise, you can offer them a 5% to 10% discount; if they give five reliable references. Reference is so powerful because when it comes from the known people; chances of conversion are very high.

Chapter 2

Purchase Transactions-When You Spend Carefully, You Save and Increase Profits

In most of the businesses, purchase of goods or services constitutes the majority of the cost. Therefore, a slight improvement in this area can impact the profits of the company in a great manner. Here are some of the ways to increase profits.

<u>Fast Impact Areas</u>

- Terms agreed with the suppliers
- Discount Policy
- Annual Discount or Incentives

<u>Strategy</u>

- Consolidation of Purchases

Let's look at them in detail

Terms agreed with the Suppliers

Generally, when the order is placed on the vendors, terms such as payment terms, delivery terms, and product quality is well documented. Herein lies the opportunity to examine purchase transactions concerning such terms and see whether there is scope for avoiding cost or recovering.

For example, in international operations, it is common for the terms like Exworks, CIF to be used. These conditions play a critical role in determining which party takes the responsibility of paying insurance and transport. Quite often this point is missed, and the businesses pay the cost which it is not supposed to pay. For example, for few of our clients, we found such occurrences and saved them lot of money.

Case Study 2.1

How a Purchase Order Term helped our client to recover 0.8 Million in Freight and Insurance

Background: This client was in the business of manufacturing forged parts and had a plant in Bangalore. It used to procure raw material from the South Korea on a continuous basis. Since it was an international transaction, delivery terms and other conditions were established. We were called on to examine to check whether cost incurred by our client was in line with the agreed terms with the supplier.

What We Did: This transaction was not straightforward, as purchase was handled by the purchasing department whereas logistics was dealt with by a different department and finally we had to check how transport and insurance costs were accounted.

As per arrangement with the supplier, it was responsible for delivering the material till factory. So we looked at documents such as Bill of entry, delivery challan, clearing and forwarding bill. We found that supply only cleared the material till Chennai. Our client incurred the transport charges from Chennai to Bangalore.

Results: We listed down all such transactions and quantified the impact of it. It came close to 0.8 million. Subsequently, vendor paid the amount by adjusting in the next bill.

Cont ...

What We Can Learn From This: Have the master sheet of all the purchase orders agreed with your suppliers. Information can be organized in the spreadsheet or can be customised in ERP or accounting software.

Case Study 2.2

How a Small Change in the Purchase Price Saved Company 1.2 Million

Background: This client was in the business of manufacturing automotive parts. Majority of the parts were made up of Steel where the price fluctuated quite a lot. Therefore, the purchasing department had to issue a purchase order to suppliers for a future period too. However, if the price decreased, Purchase order was amended retrospectively, and supplier had to issue a credit note

What We Did: As the volume of transactions was high, we listed down all the transactions for which there was an amendment to the price retrospectively. Then we compared this amendment with the bills/credit note given by the supplier.

Results: When we completed this entire exercise, we found nine transactions where the benefit of the reduced pricing was not passed on to our client. We quantified the impact, and this came to around 1.2 Million rupees.

Discount Policy

Most of the organizations have some discount policy. Either they are documented or casually communicated to the staff. For example, in a retail business, it is quite common to have a discount policy at the product category level. Discount percentages are set at product master level in an ERP or accounting software.

Just imagine that if these inputs are set wrong in the software. It can lead to massive losses in the company.

Action to be taken: So if you are in the business where discounting is common, check your discount master data.

Annual Discount or Incentives

Most of the suppliers offer bulk discount or incentives at the end of the year. However, we find it quite surprising that most of the businesses tend to forget this part of the deal and in the process, lose a lot of money.

If you can plug this loop, then you can save a substantial amount of money and increase your bottom-line.

Action to be taken: Revisit all the contracts for all the bulk purchases you never know, you might stumble upon a gold mine of money which was hidden.

Strategy –
Consolidation of Purchase

When it comes to procurement, most of the companies are not organized. In our experience, we have seen our clients buying sporadically without any planning. Thereby losing the opportunity to save cost, efficiently plan the fulfilment.

For example one of our clients was losing close to 2.4 Million because of non-planning.

Also, a lot of suppliers supply similar kind of items, in such scenario, all such purchases can be consolidated and procured from few vendors and price can be renegotiated. This again will save lot of money

Case Study 2.3

How Correcting a Purchasing Pattern Saved Solar Company INR 2.4 million

Background: This client was engaged in the business of manufacturing solar water heaters and other renewable energy products. Despite good sales numbers, our client was not making profits. We were called in to help them to increase their profits.

What We Did: As part of our profitability increase exercise, we looked at purchase pattern of the main products which constituted at least 25% of total purchase value

Results: One of the major items which our client bought was batteries. Most of the times, it was bought on ad-hoc and from different suppliers. We then questioned the purchasing department, and they had no clue. Then we suggested buying from few providers and with better planning. In next one-year company saved close to INR 2.4 Million and a result of this our client will save massive amount of money in future years

What We Can Learn From This: Identify all the purchase transactions, where sporadic purchases take place, evaluate whether such purchases can be planned. If yes, then identify the right supplier and negotiate a price which can be valid for three months, six months or year.

Chapter 3

Working Capital Management

"Earning is easy than Managing", effective management of fund helps a business to run smoothly and add more profit.

Working capital is **Current Asset – Current Liabilities**.

In simple term, working capital is **Receivables – Payables**.

All business activities are interlinked and end with either payables or receivables.

It is advisable to identify all the activities and reduce the time gap so that working capital management becomes smooth.

We have identified general events which typically fall in the working capital cycle. Bigger the cycle more working capital problem and vice versa.

Activities which affects the working capital cycle are

- Procurement
- Conversion/Despatch /Delivery
- Collection
- Payments

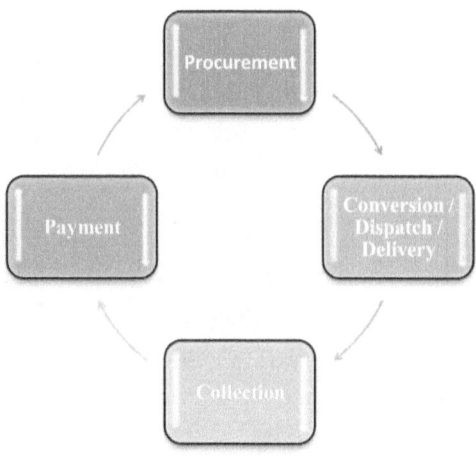

Procurement:

The time taken between placing an order and receiving goods should be reduced to bring down the working capital cycle. Time gap can be reduced with detailed planning and identifying the issues to minimise the time gaps. One can employ a lot of strategies to cut down the time. For example, signing contract with vendors for a year, issuing open PO.

Conversion/Dispatch/Delivery:

Converting raw material into finished goods, dispatching those goods, involves a lot of interlinked activities. One has to identify all the events in the process and identify the activities which can be reduced so that it takes less time to convert raw material into finished goods and subsequent processes.

Collection:

Every business wants to reduce the average collection days. There are number of strategies one can implement to reduce the collection period

Advance Receipt: Have a strategy that encourages a customer to pay in advance. For example, a bonus product or a service can be bundled with the existing one if a customer pays in advance.

Cash Discount: Offer cash discount for paying the amount before the due date. The policy of cash discount should be such that it attracts the customer to pay early and it is better to have discount rates based on the number of days.

For instance, the standard credit period is 30days then cash discount can be 3% one who pays for ten days, 2% one who pays within 20days and 0.5% one who pays within 30days.

Payment:

Reducing the average payable days will help effective management of working capital. Yes you read it right, making vendor payments early or within due date has following benefits:

Better Service: Vendors will consider you as their valuable customer, and will provide better service and try not losing you. It helps to reduce procurement time.

Better price: Making early payment helps to get a better price from suppliers. There are a lot of other indirect benefits like, on time supply, reduced inventory cost, as lot of inventory need not be carried.

Cash Flow Management:

One of the critical activities in working capital is cash flow management. Businesses need to have detailed cash flow statement.

Cash flow statement should have the clear projection of minimum 12 months and should able to know a year in advance in a particular week, how much shortage or excess of cash will be available. With such kind of projection, a business owner will be in a better position to plan the deficit or plan alternative investment of the excess fund.

Cash Flow can be projected with quite a bit of accuracy for 12 months. When preparing cash flow, business expenses have to be divided by fixed, semi-fixed and variable.

All fixed costs will be one part of the cash flow, and semi-variables will be another part. However, variable cost, which proportionately varies with the revenue, will become part of cash inflow.

Case Study 3.1
End of Struggle to Pay Suppliers and Employee on Time

Background: This Client was in the business of executing industrial projects. The client was in deep working capital problem. They were not able to pay their suppliers and employees on time. Every month-end they struggled to arrange the fund for salary payments. Management was spending their entire month in arranging funds to pay salary or clear the supplier's payments to whom PDC's (Post Dated Cheque) were issued.

What We Did: We prepared detailed projected day wise cash flow statement for first three months. The cash flow statement was divided into Cash-Inflow and Cash-Outflow. The inflow section was populated with the collection numbers expected from the future sales and existing receivables. The outflow section was populated with numbers where payments need to be done immediately and where payments could be stretched or delayed.

Results: This exercise helped in assessing shortage of cash on a particular day and helped to prepare the action plan to manage the shortage of funds proactively. Consequently, collections team started following-up aggressively for the payments. This brought to light the reasons why the payments were not made in time, like non-delivery of products on time. Subsequently, a robust process was designed to avoid such issues in future.

Chapter 4

Spend Wisely on Sales and Marketing Activities and See How Your Business Grows

Sales and Marketing department in any business is like an engine which carries the entire business. Without it, most of the businesses cannot survive.

If you have a successful marketing campaign, it can bring riches to your business in no time. On another hand, if it is done without measuring the results, then it can burn a big hole in your bank account.

It is very sad to see most of the businesses spending money blindly. Therefore, if you have good control of marketing and sales function, then you can increase profits in your business quite rapidly.

Fast Impact Areas

- Change the bidding method
- Focus on local marketing rather than generic SEO
- Measure the Sales and Marketing Effort

Change The Bidding Method

If you are doing paid advertising and you have good click-through rates, then it makes sense to change the bidding method from CPC (Cost per Click) to CPM (Cost per Impressions). The reason why we are suggesting this change is that generally, CPM rates are quite low compared to CPC.

After making this change, you will spend less money for the same number of clicks.

Action to be taken: Go to Facebook, Google AdWords Manager or any other advertising interface, run the campaign report and find out the click-through rates, if the rates are high, then change the bidding method from CPC to CPM for two-three days. If this works out well, continue with it as you will be spending less to get the same number of clicks.

Focus on Local Marketing not Generic SEO

It is quite easy to be sucked into SEO game. It takes a lot of time and effort to be really successful at it. In our experience most of our clients, who operate locally try to rank for generic keywords instead of location-based keywords.

For example: if you are selling solar water heater in Bangalore, then it is much better to go after keywords such as "Solar Water heater suppliers in Bangalore", "Best Solar Water Heaters in Bangalore", rather than competing on a national level.

Action to be taken: Optimize the website for local search terms rather than for generic search terms. If you are not good at it hire a local SEO expert, it will pay huge dividends in the long run.

Measure the Sales and Marketing Effort

This one is a no-brainer, but still, we see a lot of business not doing it. They spend money on marketing and sales without any purpose.

If you can take control of this, you can add lots of money to your bottom-line. For example, one of our clients was into selling baby products online. They heavily advertised on Google and Facebook. When we measured their results, it was quite staggering to know that Google outperformed Facebook, but our client continued spending on Facebook.

When we reported this finding to them, they said ***"We are advertising to generate awareness about our brand".***

Action to be taken: Make a list of the advertising platforms, from where you are getting the sales or leads and if possible break it down at a campaign level. Compare the sales value or number of leads generated by marketing spend, now calculate the ROI (Return on Investment). See which one is performing better.

Scale up spend on platforms which are performing better or cut down spend or simply stop the campaigns which are not giving you the desired results.

Chapter 5

Why You Should Not See Taxman As Your Enemy- He Can Also Make You Rich

There are specific tax provisions that can cut down your tax expense by 30% on year to year basis.

(Please note that some of the tax provisions discussed here only apply, if you operate your business under Indian Taxes system, but having said that there are similar rules in your countries. For more details, you can contact your local tax attorney or accountant)

Fast Impact Areas

(The list below is not exhaustive; there are certain provisions which apply to only certain businesses, therefore not included.)

- Slash Corporate Income Tax by almost 30% when you hire an employee.
- Bills you pay add money to your bank account.
- When you train or develop skills for your employees, you pay 50% tax less.

- When you export goods or services get additional benefit up to 5% of total export value.
- Technology based start-ups get tax exemption up to three years.

Slash Corporate Income Tax by Almost 30% When You Hire an Employee

In most of the businesses, people cost is a significant element in the cost structure. In manufacturing and trading, this ranges between 5-20%, whereas in software and services companies this constitutes close to 75-80%.

So it's quite clear that for the business to be profitable, people cost has to be carefully looked at. Failing so could endanger the survival of the business.

In this context, would like to bring to your notice income tax provision that can cut down the tax expense by almost 25-30%. This has been made effective from the financial year 2016-2017. This will translate in following:

- Less Pay-out of Corporate Income Tax.
- Increase in Profits after taxes.
- Increase in Shareholder's Value.

To avail the benefit of the section you need to check following:

a) If you have started the business, then you can claim this benefit for all the new employees for that financial year.

b) If you are running an existing business, then there should be an increase in the number of staff compared to previous year. For example: if the number of employees in the financial year 2015-2016 was 25 and then in the financial year 2016-2017 it increased to 30, then the benefit will be available for 5 employees. Further conditions to be satisfied are

- The employees should have worked for at least 240 days a year.
- The salary per month should not exceed INR 25000 per month.
- The employees should be enrolled in a PF program.
- The business of the company should fall under Tax-Audit under Income Tax Act.

So let us understand this benefit in little bit of detail

Company ABCD had 50 employees in the financial year 2015-2016 and 2016-2017, the number of employees increased to 65 employees. All employees of the company were enrolled in PF and company turnover exceeded INR 25 Million in financial year 2016-2017.

Employee cost of 15 employees for the financial year 2016-2017 was around 4 Million. Also, these employees worked for 240 days a year. Therefore, the company can take benefit of the provision.

So the company in the financial year 2016-2017 will get the added benefit of INR 1.2 Million (40 Lacs*30%). This benefit of 1.2 Million will continue through to 2018-2019. So in the total company will get total benefit of 3.6 Million.

So if the business falls under 30% tax bracket, the total tax saving will be around 0.37 Million each year, and for three years it will be around 1.1 Million.

Point to be noted: If the company makes losses during the year, then the benefit cannot be availed.

Bills You Pay Add Money to Bank Account

Many times expenses are paid either through a personal bank account or via credit card and later those are booked as business expenses. However, most of the time bills are taken from suppliers in personal name rather than of a business name.

This way there is loss of GST of 12-28% as input tax credit is not claimed

Examples of such expenditure are:

- Hotel Bills
- Travel Bills
- Google AdWords bills
- Telephone Postpaid bills and much more.

Below is the case study where one of our clients saved 0.3 Million by taking the bills in business name.

Case Study 5.1

How the Overhead Expenses and Capex Increased the Profitability

Background: This client was in the business of providing transport as well as warehousing services to its customers. It had to incur a lot of administrative as well as Capex spend to serve its clients. We were called in to examine whether it was availing the tax benefit on all it spends.

What We Did: We listed all such expenses were tax credit could have been taken such as advertising, sponsorship, admin, office and Capex expenses.

> **Results:** We found that most of the costs like office and admin were incurred by the employees and was claimed by them as reimbursement. Also, these bills were in their name rather than business name. We quantified the impact of this, and we concluded that company had missed out of credit of 0.3 Million. Going forward, our client made compulsory to take all the invoices in the name of the business to take credit.
>
> Another thing we found that the company did not claim tax credit available on the purchase of fixed assets. Fortunately, we were able to claim this credit. This saved company close to INR 0.7 million

When You Train Your Employees-You Save Tax Upto 50%

It is common for the companies to train or develop skills for their employees. Some of them do in-house, or some have a separate training institute for developing the skills.

Do you know you get additional deduction of 50% when you train your employees?

For example: if you incur INR 100 thousand on skill development, then you can get INR 150 thousand as tax- deductible expense. This means you have to pay less corporate income tax.

Following conditions should be satisfied to claim this benefit:

- The skill development should be for specified services and for developing skills for manufacturing of articles. Most of the services or articles manufactured by the businesses qualify for this incentive.
- Skill development should be in a separate training institute.
- The skill development program should be approved by authorities.

When You Export-You Get Additional Benefit Up To 5%

Do you know apart from the exemption of GST while exporting of goods or services, you get additional incentive whereby you get duty scripts upto the value of 5% of export value. This means you can add extra 5% to the profits when you export a good or service.

These duty scripts are freely transferable and can be used to make payment of taxes while importing of goods or services.

Also, you get the refund of indirect taxes used in the export of services or good, if they remain unutilised. One of our clients got refund of 0.42 million.

Case Study 5.2

0.42 Million of Tax Credit on Exports not availed by the Client

Background: Client was engaged in the business of providing analytic solutions to US clients. The business was completely people driven.

In the process of providing the services, the client used to incur a lot of expenses locally like telephone, consultant, travel, internet, and technical fees on which it paid taxes. We were called in to study whether all the tax benefits applicable to business were taken or not.

What We Did: As a process, we listed down all the tax benefits relevant to the client by segregating various cost and the related revenue. Almost 100% of the business was international; such services would typically qualify as export of services. When you export a service, you do not have to pay tax. This resulted in non-utilization of the tax credit which was paid on using services like telephone, travel, and internet. Since the tax credit was not utilized, our client could claim for the refund for taxes and increase their profits.

Results: To our surprise, the client had not claimed for the refund of taxes. When we inquired, client responded that they were not aware of such provision. Then we organized all the information, and guided the client to apply for the refund of taxes. The net result of this exercise resulted in the savings to the tune of INR 0.42 million. In our estimate, going forward client would be saving close to 0.55-0.60 million on year to year basis.

Starting a New Business Can Save a Ton of Tax

Do you know when you start a business which is technology based you do not have to pay corporate income tax for three years?

Most of the companies pay taxes in the range of 25-30%. When you do not pay taxes, profits increase naturally.

Apart from this, you get benefits in the forms of one-stop compliance, easy access to investment and so much more.

Some of the conditions to be satisfied to meet this condition are

- The **new** company formed should not be the result of the restructuring of the existing business.
- Technology should drive the business. So let's say if you are starting a trading or manufacturing business, then these will not qualify.
- The concerned authorities should approve it.

Chapter 6

Other Areas of Savings

When You Barter You Profit

You can use bartering to significant effect to reduce your overheads. You can do following:

a) Make list of all vendors/customers you do business. Then categorize by the business.

b) Now you make the list of services or goods you provide.

Now evaluate, whether you can transact with your vendors/customers in a way by getting in return access to the product or service which you desire. This way you can save money as there is no outflow of cash.

Example

Let's say you are Software Development Company who develops and customizes the client's software according to client's needs and want to expand your business further.

However, you do not have enough resources to expand. For expansion, you need additional computers and laptops. Then what do you do? You can use bartering to your advantage.

You can go to your existing supplier of laptops and use this script.

"If I understand your business correctly, then you supply computers/leases to companies like us and as I understand the volume of these transactions could be huge. First of all, I would like to congratulate you for doing this kind of volume. You know that I have been associated with you for years. I really care about you and your business.

Therefore, I want to ensure that you have enough internal controls in your business so that you can fully reap the rewards of your efforts. I want to help you. I will develop software that will remind you when the payment is due from your customers, when the lease expires and various other benefits.

Having said this, you would appreciate that developing such a software would require time and effort from our side. So, I need a favor from you. Can you supply me ..... no of laptops/computers as I am in the process of expanding my business. In return, I will develop you software that you can use for your lifetime, and all the updates will be free of cost to you."

Again, above example is bartering in action, you need to understand what exactly your vendor needs and modify your conversation accordingly. You can use your own creativity to come up with further ideas.

Telephone/Lease Line Bills-How to Identify Overbilling and Save Costs

Business Phone bills can be a little complex. Typically, these bills are for local service, long distance, and wireless and internet access.

Most of the companies do not look at their telephone bill carefully because it constitutes a small portion of the expenses. Mind you if you can cut down your telephone cost by 20%, it will have a bearing on your bottom-line. This becomes more significant if a company has offices in multiple locations or multiples telephone numbers for it employees.

If one carefully reviews the bill, there could be saving up to 50% on existing cost. Most of the over-billing can be detected if one looks at bill promptly.

List of Unused lines or numbers: This one is quite common, this typically happens when the employee leaves the company, then the HR or admin forgets to deactivate the number.

The actual rate of service is higher than the agreed rate: Again, this can be detected if the month to month comparison is made and the master database of all the approved rates is kept in one place.

Action Steps to be taken:

- Make the database of all the numbers, lines, and internet access with agreed rates.

- Review and compare the charged amount to agreed rate.

- When employee leaves, immediately the notice should go to the service provider to deactivate the number.

- Most of the offices have EPBX system, try to have maintenance done on the requirement basis rather than an annual maintenance contract.

Travel Expense-Things to Do to Save Cost

Travel expenses present great opportunity to enhance profitability as this expense can be controlled easily.

Action Steps to be Taken

Aggregate all the related expenses together: Aggregate the information by airline cost, hotels, car lease. Use this information with the vendors to arrive at the corporate discount.

Corporate Credit Card: In most companies, employees use their personal credit card for travel expense. However, the benefits in the form of reward points accrue to them rather than the company. The reward points can be later used for redemption of air-tickets, dining, and other benefits

Have a Clear-Cut Travel Policy: It is good practice to have standard rates for the reimbursement of fuel, hotel rates, and other expenses. This will ensure that expenses are uniform and are well within the budgets of the company.

Do you want to increase business profits quickly? Then book your free consultation session with the authors by logging into the website

http://www.soatech.in/24hr-business-turnaround/

Bonus Chapter

What You Can Learn From Competitors

Today most of the businesses are competing quite hard to get the same customer. Therefore, you should know what your competitors are doing, attracting the customer.

You can do the following to track and learn from your competitors:

The key to any online business is to have targeted traffic to the website. Below are tool and resources, you can use to analyze competitors traffic.

Alexa.com: It gives you the website ranking and overview of the traffic details.

Semrush.com: This tool is a killer, it gives you data on parameters like paid keywords, keywords used for SEO, ads that your competitors are running and much more.

Moz.com: It gives you insights on the organic traffic with details on the backlinks.

Google AdWords: AdWords has this feature where you can get keyword ideas. In the keyword section, just put competitor's website. In turn,

Google will throw up the keywords which your competitors might be using for online campaigns.

Website: Most of the websites contains client list. When you browse the client list, you will get a fair idea what type of clients your competitors market to.

Process: If your competitor has a sales funnel, you can sign up and see what kind of emails they send to engage their subscribers. You can learn a lot from this and if required implement in your campaigns.

Expenses Add Profits to Your Bank Account

Some expenses add profits to your business.

These expenses only come into picture when there are sales. So, more the variable expenses, more the profitability. The key is to have a cost model in a business which has more variable expenses then fixed expenses. So the obvious question is how to convert expenses into variable one and reduce fixed costs.

Below are the tips:

Salary Expenses: it is quite common to have a compensation structure, without taking into account, the performance attached to it. It is recommended that salary structure should comprise of fixed plus variable element, and the variable should always be linked to some performance.

Performance could be in terms of increased sales, number of leads generated, feedback from clients, completing the task on time and list can go on.

When you do this, two things happen. First, you know the employee you have hired, is capable one and willing to take challenges and second, you know for sure that you have only to pay when a defined performance takes place.

Marketing Expenses: Even though marketing is closely connected to sales. Most of the times it is fixed in nature, as the results take time to show up.

In the process, fixed salary cost and cost towards Google, Facebook Ads and other marketing activities are incurred without corresponding increase in sales. This can take a heavy toll on the bottom-line.

In this scenario, it makes sense to outsource the marketing activities instead of doing in-house.

For example, database creation can be outsourced to freelancers. Videos, Logos and other marketing collaterals can be outsourced to competent workers on Fiverr or Odesk.com. Cold Calls can be outsourced to a company or freelancer who charges on hourly basis or number of calls made. This way you make your business more flexible and expandable.

Office and Admin Expenses: Typically these include rent, HR, accountant and compliance cost. For example, sometimes the office is not used to its full capacity. In that case, you can share the office space with another company and reduce fixed rent cost. HR and accounting activities can be outsourced, as you pay only for the work done.

Is Your Business Suffering From Feast or Famine Cycle?

It is very common for a business to undergo feast and famine cycles. There are phases when business makes lots of money and times there no money.

The reason for it is pretty obvious; there is no predictable revenue system built in the business. Most of the business owners believe that customers will keep coming as it has been a trend. The moment there is a lull they start implementing which we call "Instant Gratification Method".

The knee jerk reaction is to execute campaigns or activities like email campaigns, speaking to old customers or acquaintances, which will generate leads and some will convert into sales, and again they fall into old patterns.

"On another hand, successful businesses have the mentality that if we invest 10k per month in marketing, it will generate 25 leads and 10 sales". Based on this model they plan the revenue numbers and calibrate the marketing efforts accordingly.

Now the obvious question is how you build such systems?

Below are the steps you can start implementing to build such system

- Define Your Ideal Customer.
- Define the Medium to Reach the Customer.
- Identify the Buying Stage of Your Customer: There are typically four stages of buying.

First is Indifferent stage- At this stage, the customer is oblivious to your product or service.

Second is Curiosity Stage: At this stage, customers are curious to know more about the product or services you have to offer.

Third is sitting on the Fence Stage. At this stage, the customer has taken a proposal from three to four vendors.

Fourth is Sold on The Offer Stage. At this stage, the customer is willing to buy the product or service from you.

- **Build Lead Magnets for Different Stages:** It could be building a landing page or identifying referral partners or channels, which will bring leads.

  Let's say you are an Interior Designer. You want to target homeowners who have just moved in, and looking for an interior designer. **(They are right now in curiosity stage).** In this scenario, you can build a landing page whereby you can capture the homeowners contact details. In exchange for contact details, you give a free report which says **"7 Things You Need to Know Before You Engage an Interior Designer".** Once they are into your sales funnel, you can follow-up or nurture based on their buying stage.

- **Measuring the Effort:** You should clearly know which source is giving you the number of leads and at what cost. This will help you to ascertain customer acquisition cost and which lead sources are working best.

About the Authors

Govind is perhaps India's one of the finest young financial management brains. He was honoured and recognized by Economic Times in "Power of Ideas Summit", a few years ago. He has around 12+ years of experience in the F&A strategy and Optimisation. He has rich experience of working with some of the biggest companies in India and abroad.

Currently, he is spearheading the Virtual CFO services of the Soatech Solution.

He can be reached at govindaraju.tv@soatech.in

Sharad Churiwala has rich experience in Accounting and Financial reporting having worked in Fortune 500 companies

He currently advises business owners across the world on how to improve their business in the field of finance and marketing, and spearheads the Enterprise Profit Optimisation services at Soatech Solution.

He can be reached at sharad@soatech.in

Sharad and Govind have also co-authored the book **"Five Simple Ways to Save Cost in Business"**

About Soatech

Soatech Solution Private Limited is an integrated Finance & Management consulting company; providing Service in India and abroad. Soatech core competency lies in understanding the dynamics of a wide range of business, and providing tailored made solutions to address the specific needs of clients.

We offer turnkey solutions right from providing initial strategic, and legal support to set up a company, to financial management, to help businesses establish management review system that captures the key performance deliverables in the company. Hence, we aim to create value for every node of the company's value chain with the aim of creating a self-serving business model aiding companies in optimizing their resources more efficiently.

> Do you want to increase business profits quickly? Then book your free consultation session with the authors by logging into the website
>
> http://www.soatech.in/24hr-business-turnaround/

Compendium of Case Studies

Case Study 1.1
Error in Cash Discount-Company had to Pay
0.21 Million

Background: Client was in the business of selling and buying garments. We were engaged to look at the existing process on discounting and billing and internal controls for financial transactions.

What We Did: We took the sales register for one year. Against the sales, we plotted the received amount. We then calculated number of days to receive the payment invoice wise. We also added a column, where cash discount was given. Then we looked at the report for the correctness of Cash discount.

Results: Finally, it was concluded that the company paid close to excess of INR 0.21 Million. When we reported this to the client, then client agreed to it saying it was attributable to manual systems and lack of proper control. Basically, the system of giving cash discount was not formalized. Post this; we set up a discount master data in the accounting software at the customer level. So the moment there was an error in cash discount, the software sent out the alerts to responsible parties in the company. Since this company had a large volume of sales on daily basis, a review mechanism to review the cash discount on weekly basis was setup.

Also for excess cash discount of INR 0.21 Million was subsequently recovered from the customers via debit note. With this information in hand, we also looked at cash flow statement of the client on month to month basis. Cash discount was given to plug the gap between the receivables and payables, and at times it was not necessary to really give a Cash discount. Mind you our client was giving on an average of 2% Cash Discount. We estimated that if the client had managed Cash Flow well, it could have avoided 0.202 Million of Cash Discount.

What We Can Learn from this: It's a good idea to review the cash discount calculations on a monthly basis

Case Study 2.1
How a Purchase Order Term helped our client to recover 0.8 Million in Freight and Insurance

Background: This client was in the business of manufacturing forged parts and had a plant in Bangalore. It used to procure raw material from the South Korea on a continuous basis. Since it was an international transaction, delivery terms and other conditions were established. We were called on to examine to check whether cost incurred by our client was in line with the agreed terms with the supplier.

What We Did: This transaction was not straightforward, as purchase was handled by the purchasing department whereas logistics was dealt with by a different department and finally we had to check how transport and insurance costs were accounted.

As per arrangement with the supplier, it was responsible for delivering the material till factory. So we looked at documents such as Bill of entry, delivery challan, clearing and forwarding bill. We found that supply only cleared the material till Chennai. Our client incurred the transport charges from Chennai to Bangalore.

Results: We listed down all such transactions and quantified the impact of it. It came close to 0.8 million. Subsequently, vendor paid the amount by adjusting in the next bill.

What We Can Learn From This: Have the master sheet of all the purchase orders agreed with your suppliers. Information can be organized in the spreadsheet or can be customised in ERP or accounting software.

Case Study 2.2
How a Small Change in the Purchase Price
Saved Company 1.2 Million

Background: This client was in the business of manufacturing automotive parts. Majority of the parts were made up of Steel where the price fluctuated quite a lot. Therefore, the purchasing department had to issue a purchase order to suppliers for a future period too. However, if the price decreased, Purchase order was amended retrospectively, and supplier had to issue a credit note

What We Did: As the volume of transactions was high, we listed down all the transactions for which there was an amendment to the price retrospectively.

Then we compared this amendment with the bills/credit note given by the supplier.

Results: When we completed this entire exercise, we found nine transactions where the benefit of the reduced pricing was not passed on to our client. We quantified the impact, and this came to around 1.2 Million rupees.

Case Study 2.3
How Correcting a Purchasing Pattern Saved Solar Company INR 2.4 million

Background: This client was engaged in the business of manufacturing solar water heaters and other renewable energy products. Despite good sales numbers, our client was not making profits. We were called in to help them to increase their profits.

What We Did: As part of our profitability increase exercise, we looked at purchase pattern of the main products which constituted at least 25% of total purchase value

Results: One of the major items which our client bought was batteries. Most of the times, it was bought on ad-hoc and from different suppliers. We then questioned the purchasing department, and they had no clue. Then we suggested buying from few providers and with better planning. In next one-year company saved close to INR 2.4 Million and a result of this our client will save massive amount of money in future years

What We Can Learn From This: Identify all the purchase transactions, where sporadic purchases take place, evaluate whether such purchases can be planned. If yes, then identify the right supplier and negotiate a price which can be valid for three months, six months or year.

Case Study 3.1
End of Struggle to Pay Suppliers and Employee on Time

Background: This Client was in the business of executing industrial projects. The client was in deep working capital problem. They were not able to pay their suppliers and employees on time. Every month-end they struggled to arrange the fund for salary payments. Management was spending their entire month in arranging funds to pay salary or clear the supplier's payments to whom PDC's (Post Dated Cheque) were issued.

What We Did: We prepared detailed projected day wise cash flow statement for first three months. The cash flow statement was divided into Cash-Inflow and Cash-Outflow. The inflow section was populated with the collection numbers expected from the future sales and existing receivables. The outflow section was populated with numbers where payments need to be done immediately and where payments could be stretched or delayed.

Results: This exercise helped in assessing shortage of cash on a particular day and helped to prepare the action plan to manage the shortage of funds proactively. Consequently, collections team started following-up aggressively for the payments. This brought to light the reasons why the payments were not made in time, like non-delivery of products on time. Subsequently, a robust process was designed to avoid such issues in future.

Case Study 5.1
How the Overhead Expenses and Capex Increased the Profitability

Background: This client was in the business of providing transport as well as warehousing services to its customers. It had to incur a lot of administrative as well as Capex spend to serve its clients. We were called in to examine whether it was availing the tax benefit on all it spends.

What We Did: We listed all such expenses were tax credit could have been taken such as advertising, sponsorship, admin, office and Capex expenses.

Results: We found that most of the costs like office and admin were incurred by the employees and was claimed by them as reimbursement. Also, these bills were in their name rather than business name. We quantified the impact of this, and we concluded that company had missed out of credit of 0.3 Million. Going forward, our client made compulsory to take all the invoices in the name of the business to take credit.

Another thing we found that the company did not claim tax credit available on the purchase of fixed assets. Fortunately, we were able to claim this credit. This saved company close to INR 0.7 million

Case Study 5.2
0.42 Million of Tax Credit on Exports not availed by the Client

Background: Client was engaged in the business of providing analytic solutions to US clients. The business was completely people driven.

In the process of providing the services, the client used to incur a lot of expenses locally like telephone, consultant, travel, internet, and technical fees on which it paid taxes. We were called in to study whether all the tax benefits applicable to business were taken or not.

What We Did: As a process, we listed down all the tax benefits relevant to the client by segregating various cost and the related revenue. Almost 100% of the business was international; such services would typically qualify as export of services. When you export a service, you do not have to pay tax. This resulted in non-utilization of the tax credit which was paid on using services like telephone, travel, and internet. Since the tax credit was not utilized, our client could claim for the refund for taxes and increase their profits.

Results: To our surprise, the client had not claimed for the refund of taxes. When we inquired, client responded that they were not aware of such provision. Then we organized all the information, and guided the client to apply for the refund of taxes. The net result of this exercise resulted in the savings to the tune of INR 0.42 million. In our estimate, going forward client would be saving close to 0.55-0.60 million on year to year basis.

www.ingramcontent.com/pod-product-compliance
Lightning Source LLC
Chambersburg PA
CBHW030501220526
45464CB00006B/2612